cottage core

COTTAGECORE

Copyright © Summersdale Publishers Ltd, 2020

With text by Anna Martin, Claire Berrisford, Elanor Clarke, Sophie Martin and Vicki Vrint

An Hachette UK Company
www.hachette.co.uk

Summersdale Publishers Ltd
Part of Octopus Publishing Group Limited
Carmelite House
50 Victoria Embankment
LONDON
EC4Y 0DZ
UK

www.summersdale.com

Printed and bound in the Czech Republic

ISBN: 978-1-78783-894-9

Substantial discounts on bulk quantities of Summersdale books are available to corporations, professional associations and other organizations. For details contact general enquiries: telephone: +44 (0) 1243 771107 or email: enquiries@summersdale.com.

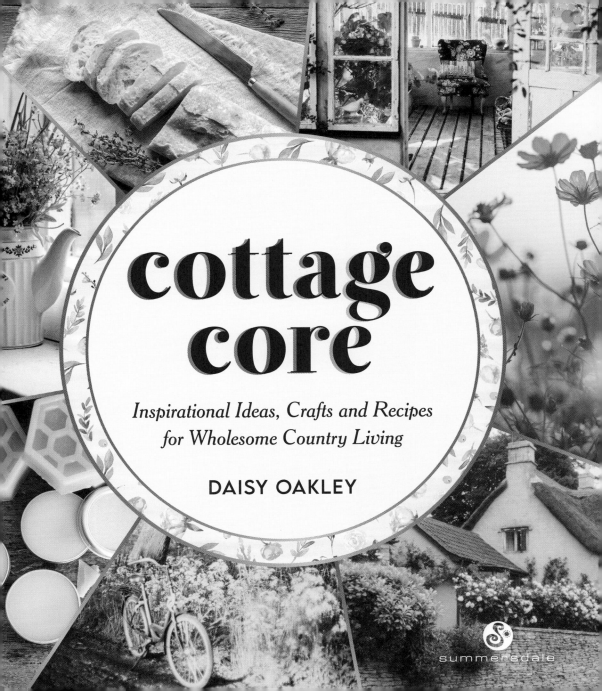

cottage core

Inspirational Ideas, Crafts and Recipes
for Wholesome Country Living

DAISY OAKLEY

summersdale

Contents

Introduction

Like so many movements, cottagecore gained popularity through social media, but in reality it exists far from technology, amongst sprawling meadows and wild gardens. It is a trend that allows all – regardless of gender, age, race or sexuality – to indulge in traditional visuals reminiscent of a simpler time. Born of a desire to return to a slower way of living, it is a movement that revels in the romance of rural life and celebrates a pastoral fantasy: think of soft, sun-faded aprons and the scent of freshly baked bread and you're halfway there.

If you're looking to live a life that evokes the countryside dream but reside far from the wilderness, fear not. It's never been simpler to evoke dreamy homestead vibes, no matter where you live. From wholesome recipes and craft ideas to activities to bring you into harmony with nature, let the suggestions in these pages help you disconnect from modern life and live out the cottagecore fantasy.

Spring

Spring has sprung, and with it comes a burst of colour and birdsong. The longer evenings and milder temperatures make this a great time to make the most of nature, with opportunities for foraging and crafting everywhere.

We've included a host of activities to set you up for these warmer months; from soap- and candle-making to recipes for your own pantry staples, as well as ideas to get you back in the great outdoors to witness this most fascinating season unfold.

Setting the Table

A beautifully laid table need not be restricted to formal occasions, but is something that can be done every day to make all meal times special. It needn't be expensive; paper or linen napkins and a plain white tablecloth create a simple but effective result, as do freshly picked flowers from the garden in a jam jar, a spray of spring leaves or a hoard of beach finds clustered in the centre of the table.

Candles and glass provide instant ambience and sparkle. Don't strive for perfection when hosting a gathering – a simple spread of cheeses, olives and bread on a wooden board with wine, or home-baked buns, show that you've put love and care into your meal.

Scented candles
for a lovely aroma

Flowers from
the garden

11

Elderflower Fritters

2-3 heads per person

This fragrant treat makes a delicious dessert. Be sure to pluck the heads when the buds have just flowered for the best flavour.

Preparation time
20 minutes

Cooking time
2 minutes per head

Ingredients
15 elderflower heads

100 g plain flour

2 tbsp oil, plus a pan of oil
    for frying

175 ml sparkling water

Cold plate of icing sugar

Honey or ice cream to serve

Method

Cut the elderflower heads so there is enough stem to hold them by. Shake off any little bugs and rinse them in cold water.

Sift the flour into a bowl and stir in the oil and water.

Heat the pan of oil until it sizzles when you flick a tiny drop of water into it.

Hold the elderflowers by their stems and dunk them into the batter mix, then push them headfirst into the oil.

Fry for 1–2 minutes until batter is golden and crisp, then hold them first on some kitchen roll to soak the excess oil and then on the plate of caster sugar.

Serve hot with ice cream or a drizzle of honey.

Bunting

Home-made bunting is a quick and fun way to bring a party feel to any indoor space. It creates a gorgeous border in a room and adds a touch of rustic charm. It's easy to make and you can use all sorts of odds and ends to create your bunting – scraps of paper, pieces of fabric, old clothes and even plastic and paper bags. Unleash your creative side and have a craft day at home.

What you'll need

Thin cardboard

Pretty material and fabrics

Glue, or needle and thread

Ribbon, string or twine

Drawing pins to hang the bunting (optional)

Scissors

Instructions

- Make a triangle template out of card.

- Use the template to cut lots of triangles from your chosen material (wintry designs, such as snowflakes, icicles and pine trees, work well, as do warm patterns, such as tartan).

- Glue or stitch the triangles to a length of ribbon, string or rustic twine.

- The trickiest part of the whole process is choosing where to hang your bunting! It looks great in bedrooms and adds a quirky edge to kitchens and living rooms. You can hang it on walls, attach it to shelves, or use it as a garland for a mantelpiece – just be careful it's not too near the fire.

- Once you've hung your bunting, invite some friends round to admire your handiwork (this is the perfect excuse for a night of board games, drinks and nibbles!).

Bike Rides

Few activities inspire a greater sense of freedom than a bike ride. It's an excellent form of low-impact exercise and will give you a thrill as you cycle along tracks and freewheel down hills – like you used to when you were a child.

Enjoy the fresh air as it ruffles your hair and the warmth of the sun on your face. Connect with your body as you power the pedals. There's no better way to travel!

I felt my lungs inflate with the onrush of scenery ... I thought, 'This is what it is to be happy.'

Sylvia Plath

Choosing candles to decorate your home

Most candles are made from paraffin wax. Paraffin wax is a by-product of crude oil and is often mixed with additives to improve its burn rate. There are concerns that burning these candles releases air pollutants and toxic black soot into the air. However, there are alternative waxes that burn more cleanly, with less soot and smoke. Beeswax is more expensive than paraffin wax, but it is a natural wax derived from honeybees. Soy wax, from soybeans, is another alternative. Less expensive than beeswax, it may be 100 per cent soybean oil or soybean oil blended with other vegetable oils or waxes.

Don't forget to place candles outside your home too. Sitting on a balcony or patio, surrounded by flickering candles, with a steaming mug of tea or coffee is a treat that you can enjoy every day.

Essential oils

Invest in candles infused with essential oils. Aside from filling the room with beautiful aromas, essential oils can enhance our well-being, and influence our thoughts, emotions and moods. Different oils affect us in different ways. Some oils are calming, such as lavender and bergamot, and some are refreshing, such as lemon and rose. Try out some of the following if you are experiencing any of these health complaints:

- **Stress:** *lavender, bergamot, vetiver, pine and ylang-ylang*

- **Insomnia:** *lavender, camomile, jasmine, rose and sandalwood*

- **Anxiety:** *rose, clary sage, lemon, Roman camomile and sandalwood*

- **Depressed mood:** *peppermint, camomile, lavender and jasmine*

- **Memory and attention problems:** *sage, peppermint and cinnamon*

- **Low energy:** *clove, jasmine, tea tree, rosemary, sage and citrus*

Make Your Own Soap

Soap is a lovely gift and once you realize just how easy it is to make, there'll be no stopping you.

Ingredients

500 g of Castile melt
and pour soap base*

Coloured liquid soap dye
of your choice (optional)

1 tsp of essential oil of
your choice (lavender or
rose are good options)

100 ml of 90 per
cent IPA alcohol

Equipment

Sharp knife

Chopping board

Double-boiler saucepan
or a metal bowl (or
a heatproof jug and
a microwave)

Metal spoon

Soap mould with
500-g capacity

* Melt and pour soap
base is available in
clear, white or off-
white, so it's up to you
which one you use.

Instructions

Chop up the melt and pour soap base into 1 cm (0.4 in.) cubes and place into a double boiler or a metal bowl over a saucepan of boiling water or into a heatproof jug to go into the microwave for melting.

Stir the liquid a few times with the metal spoon to make sure there are no lumps, then add a few drops of liquid soap dye (if using) and your essential oil.

Give the mixture a good stir then it's ready to pour into your mould. If using a silicone mould, you will need to place it in a sturdy container – such as a lunchbox, small tin or baking dish – to keep the silicone from warping when you pour in the soap.

Spray a thin layer of the alcohol on top of the soap as this prevents bubbles from forming and will ensure a smooth finish.

Leave the soap to harden for a couple of hours. Remove the silicone mould from the container and, before turning out the soap, give the silicone a gentle squeeze at the base just to make sure it has set properly.

Once set, turn out the soap and cut into blocks with a sharp knife.

Package up in waxed paper or parchment paper to store if not using immediately.

Cottagecore inspiration

Forest treasures: wild garlic

Wild garlic grows in forests and woody areas in most parts of the northern hemisphere from around March to June. Due to its distinctive garlic scent you can usually smell it before you see it! Spear-shaped leaves give way to small clusters of white, star-shaped flowers, and they grow in great numbers, often carpeting the forest floor. Although picking wild flowers is generally frowned upon, due to this natural abundance, the removal of a few leaves and flowers from a wide area will not have a detrimental impact.

Both the leaves and flowers of wild garlic are edible. The leaves can be eaten raw or used in sauces and soups; the flowers, which bloom later in the season, make great additions to salads. There are also many health benefits associated with this plant: as well as containing vitamins A and C, calcium and iron, and having antibacterial properties, wild garlic is said to lower cholesterol and reduce blood pressure.

To harvest, pick the leaves and flowers of wild garlic plants using scissors or secateurs. Put cuttings into a plastic bag, taking care to be gentle as the leaves can bruise easily. Refrigerate them once you return home and keep them for up to a week.

Note: When foraging, beware: wild garlic looks very similar to lily of the valley, which is poisonous. Before harvesting what you think is garlic, always take one leaf of the plant and crush it between your fingers. If it smells like garlic, it's safe to use.

Wild Garlic Pesto Serves 4

Ingredients

80 g wild garlic leaves
  (or more to taste)

30 g Parmesan, grated

30 g pine nuts

3 tbsp olive oil

Lemon juice, to taste

Salt and pepper

400 g fresh pasta or
  tomatoes, sliced, to serve

Method

Wash the garlic leaves thoroughly and pat dry.

Put the garlic, Parmesan, pine nuts and oil in a blender and blitz until smooth. Alternatively, crush by hand with a pestle and mortar.

Then add lemon juice, salt and pepper to taste. Add more oil if you prefer pesto with a thinner consistency.

Mix the pesto into fresh pasta and serve, or drizzle over sliced tomatoes for a zingy salad.

Drying herbs for year-round use

Sturdy herbs, such as dill, bay, rosemary and oregano, can be air-dried on a windowsill. Moisture-rich herbs, such as basil, lemon balm and mint, are best oven-dried so that they dry out more quickly to avoid mould.

Before air-drying herbs, cut and remove any dry or diseased leaves. Shake gently to remove any insects or rinse with cool water and pat dry with paper towels (wet herbs will mould and rot). Remove the lower leaves along the bottom inch or so of each branch. Bundle four to six branches together and tie as a bunch using string or a rubber band, then leave these on a windowsill or a sunny spot in the house. You can even hang them up by making a makeshift washing line and using washing pegs to keep them in place. The bundles will shrink as they dry and the rubber band will loosen, so check periodically that the bundles are not slipping.

For sturdier herbs such as rosemary, make small bundles for drying, tying the bunches together with string or a rubber band as before. Punch or cut several holes in a paper bag. Label the bag with the name of the herb to be dried and place the herb bundle upside down in the bag. Gather the ends of the bag around the bundle and tie closed. Make sure the herbs are not crowded inside the bag. Hang the bag upside down in a warm, airy room and check in about two weeks to see how things are progressing. Keep checking weekly until the herbs are dry and ready to store.

Once dried, store your herbs in airtight containers in a cool, dark place. They should remain fresh for up to two years.

Make Your Own Herbal Teabags

Making your own herbal teas will reduce both your caffeine intake and your expenditure! It's also fun mixing different herbs to create your own blends. Natural cotton drawstring teabags are simple to make and you can make a batch to store in a tin or Mason jar – they not only look beautiful but are reusable too.

Makes approx. 50 teabags

You will need

1 m² unbleached muslin

Scissors

Unbleached embroidery thread or similar (for the drawstring)

Sewing machine (or needle and thimble)

Cotton

Your fresh or dried herbs (and spices – optional)

Instructions

Create a template or use a ruler and mark out 6.5 x 7.5 cm (2.55 x 2.95 in.) oblongs on the muslin – the reason why they aren't square is to allow for the drawstring opening at the top of the bag.

When you have your cut pieces, take one piece and fold over and pin 1.5 cm (0.6 in.) at the top of the longer length to create the tunnel for the drawstring. Sew this fold in place and repeat on another fabric piece (you can use a sewing machine or hand stitch the fabric using a running stitch).

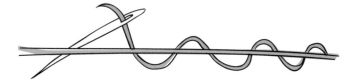

Pin these two pieces together with the raw edges facing out and carefully sew the two sides below the drawstring tunnel. Then sew along the bottom to create the bag.

Trim away some of the raw edges but be careful not to cut into the stitches.

Turn the bag right side out, so that the raw edges are on the inside of the bag.

Cut an 18 cm (7 in.) length of your cotton. Use a needle to guide this thread through the tunnel at the top of the bag. Make sure that you leave a short length at both ends for the drawstring to work effectively.

Repeat until you have used up your fabric!

- Get creative with your herb mixes. You can buy dried herbs cheaply in bulk from health food stores. Use a teaspoon each of different herbs and spices and let your taste buds and imagination run wild. Add in your fresh or dried herbs and spices – fill the bag so it's bulging!

- Your homemade teabags can be stored until needed – the fresh herbs will keep their potency even when they have dried.

- Boil some water, pick out your favourite cup, drop in a bag and pour over boiled water. Leave to infuse for a few minutes, then drink and enjoy!

To reuse your cotton teabags, clean out the used tea, then give them a rinse in water (without detergent) and leave to air-dry. If this all sounds a bit fiddly, you can purchase pre-made bags online relatively cheaply.

A lovely warm sunny morning, the purple plumes of the silver birch fast thickening with buds waved and swayed gently in the soft spring air against the deep cloudless blue sky. The apricot blossoms were blowing and under the silver weeping birch the daffodils were dancing and nodding their golden heads in the morning wind and sunshine.

—

Rev. Francis Kilvert

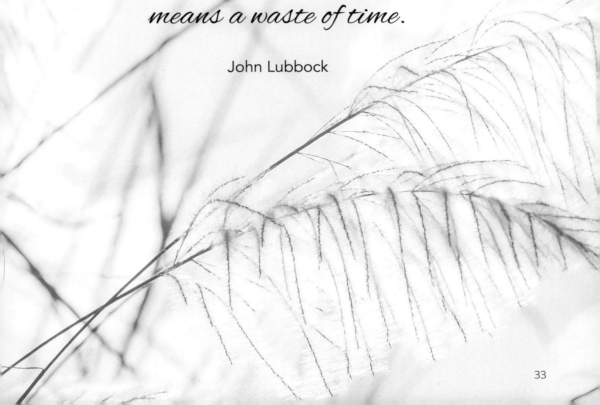

To lie sometimes on the grass under trees on a summer's day, listening to the murmur of the water, or watching the clouds float across the sky, is by no means a waste of time.

John Lubbock

Leftover roasted vegetable tart

Serves 4

This delicious tart can be made from any leftover vegetables you have to hand. With fresh herbs, this is all the flavours of spring in one tart!

Ingredients

Butter for greasing

1 roll pre-rolled
  shortcrust pastry

1 egg, beaten

Leftover vegetables

A few sprigs of fresh thyme,
  parsley or chives

Goat's cheese

Method

Preheat the oven to 180°C/350°F/Gas 4.

Grease a 22 cm diameter pie dish with the butter.

Unroll the pastry and place over the pie dish. Gently push the pastry into the base and sides. Trim the excess pastry from the edges, leaving an overhang of 2.5 cm.

Prick the base of the pastry with a fork and wash the border with the beaten egg. Bake blind for approximately five minutes.

Arrange the vegetables in the pastry case and dot with thyme and goat's cheese.

Bake for 15 minutes or until pastry is golden.

Serve hot with salad or chips.

Tip

If you're short on time but want to have a hot, nutritious meal when you get home of an evening, invest in a slow cooker. This is one-step, one-pot cooking and it couldn't be simpler. They also use less electricity than a conventional oven and with the longer low-temperature cooking time, they help to tenderize cheaper cuts of meat, as well as bringing out the flavours in food. Many meals can be created in a slow-cooker, such as stews, casseroles and soups.

Wildflower wonders

Get creative with old bits and bobs you have lying around to create a decorative planter for wildflowers or even for growing your own herbs or veggies.

Create a garden masterpiece
with a vintage typewriter

An old pair of boots makes a
cosy home for spring flowers

Repurposed tyres make robust planters for fruits and vegetables

Create hanging baskets with helmets or even flippers — the sky is the limit

Spend Time with Trees

Get in touch with nature – literally! As you walk through forest and woodland, reach out to feel the world around you: the texture of leaves, the soft petal of a flower, or perhaps the water of a stream. Particularly soothing are the trees. Even just being in their presence can have a calming effect, but it's been proven that spending a few minutes hugging a tree can bring you real health benefits too, such as reducing stress, and improving your mental well-being by giving you a sense of positivity, confidence and calm.

Wrap your arms around the trunk of a tree and link your fingers if you can. Rest your cheek against the bark, close your eyes and feel your heartbeat slow. Feel the stillness and steadiness of the tree, imagine both its roots anchored into the ground and the branches that reach upwards. Soon this feeling of being grounded will transfer to you.

Summer

The cottagecore aesthetic stems from all things natural and wild, which makes summer the ultimate season to enjoy some simple, wholesome activities. Find solace in the streaming sunlight and let the gentle hum of the bees inspire you to live life a little slower in the coming months.

Let your creativity shine by crafting displays and useful items from the best that summer has to offer, or perhaps make traditional living a reality with delicious recipes for making your own bread and beer. It's likely though that our simplest suggestion is the one we all need the most: feel the grass between your toes and gaze peacefully at the clouds as they pass you by.

Fresh Flowers

Nothing nurtures the heart and soul more than fresh flowers. Fill your home with blooms that make you feel happy – bold tulips, romantic roses and vibrant daffodils – and choose scents that make you smile, such as sweet hyacinths or fragrant lilies. Cottagecore is about cherishing yourself so don't wait for someone to buy you flowers; head to your local florist or farmers' market and treat yourself to a bunch of your favourites. Even better, pick sweet peas, lavender and peonies straight from your garden or window box. Don't worry if you don't have enough vases – you can use jugs, jam jars, glass bottles, Mason jars and even mugs. Whether it's a bouquet or a single striking stem, place the flowers where you can see them every day and they can work their magic.

Beauty without virtue is a rose without scent.

Danish proverb

Lavender Bags

What you'll need

Pretty fabric

Scissors

Pins

Needle and thread

Dried lavender

Optional extra: ribbon

Instructions

Lavender has been used for its healing properties for thousands of years and its fragrance can be relaxing and restorative. Lavender bags are easy to make and are useful in lots of different ways. Try tucking one in a drawer or wardrobe to keep your clothes and sheets smelling fresh or pop one under your pillow to encourage a peaceful night's sleep. You could even keep one in your handbag or pocket to help you to de-stress with its calming aroma when you're having a busy day.

1

Cut out two rectangles of fabric measuring 16 x 11.5 cm.

Pin the two rectangles together, patterned sides facing each other.

2

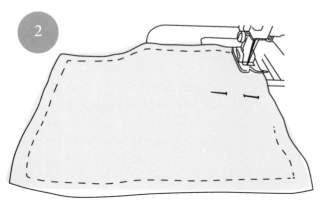

Starting about 2 cm from the edge of one of the short sides, sew all the way round the rectangle, stopping roughly 2 cm from the other corner.

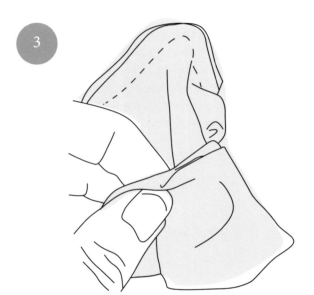

3

Cut off the corners and turn the rectangle the right way round, pushing the fabric through the gap you've left (you can use the end of a pencil or a paint brush to push out the corners so they're pointy).

4

Iron the seam across the gap so it's nice and straight.

Fill with dried lavender (you can buy this online or through a local lavender farm), or dry your own if you have access to a lavender bush.

5

If you'd like to hang up your bag, place a loop of ribbon halfway across the top edge of the gap and sew across the gap, backstitching over the ribbon to make sure it stays in place.

Ta-dah! — your own gorgeous lavender bag!

Fairy-Light Lanterns

What you'll need

1–3 large mason jars

1–3 strings of LED battery-operated fairy lights

A piece of hessian big enough to cover the battery pack

Sticking tape

Instructions

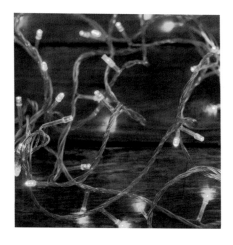

Add a little sparkle to your life by creating some fairy-light lanterns. Fairy lights are a wonderful way to create a special atmosphere. They cast a romantic, whimsical glow and add a touch of magic to any room. These lanterns take minutes to make and create a stunning backdrop for a party or to warm up a chilly spring night in.

- Take one string of fairy lights and disguise the battery pack with a small piece of hessian. Carefully drop the battery box into the bottom of a mason jar (make sure the on–off button is facing up so you can easily reach in and turn the lights off)*.

- Spread the fairy lights inside the jar so they fill the space. (You may need to use several strings of fairy lights if you are using a very large jar.)

- Tape the top of the light string to the inside of the lid and screw the lid back on the jar.

- Stand back and be dazzled by your creation.

*Alternatively, buy a string of fairy lights with a battery pack small enough to tape to the underside of the jar lid. Tie a thick ribbon or piece of fabric around the neck of the jar to hide the battery pack from view.

Solid Perfume

Make your own luxurious perfume bar – either to give as a unique present or to keep all to yourself.

Ingredients

30 g beeswax pellets

30 g sweet almond essential oil

15 drops of your desired essential oil(s) – it can be a mix of scents (such as rose and vanilla or bergamot and lemon)

Shallow glass screw-top jars to store your perfume (either reuse old ones or buy online)

Instructions

Melt the beeswax and almond oil. This can be done in either a metal or heatproof bowl over a pan of simmering water or in a microwave.

Once melted, carefully drop in your essential oils, mixing them in with a metal teaspoon.

Pour the mixture into the containers and leave to set before screwing on the lid.

The perfume works by applying it with your fingertips. The heat from your fingers liquefies the perfume, which can then be applied to your pulse points.

Experiment with different scents and varying amounts of essential oil to create your own signature scent.

Cloud Watching

They often go unnoticed, but if you take time to look up, you'll catch one of nature's most impressive and beautiful displays: the clouds. A sunny sky is often what we hope for when we're planning a day in the open, but a cloudy sky is infinitely more interesting. Every cloud is as unique as a snowflake. They are constantly evolving, and the ways they change and catch the light can create moments of striking, majestic beauty.

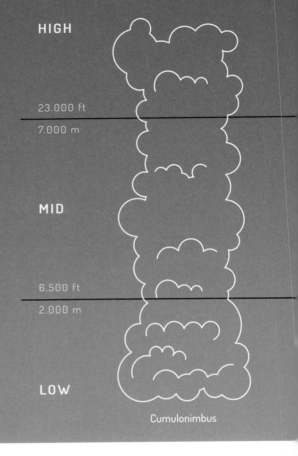

HIGH

23.000 ft
7.000 m

MID

6.500 ft
2.000 m

LOW

Cumulonimbus

A field guide to clouds

Cirrus: Thin, wispy, high-level clouds, which often appear on sunny days and at sunrise and sunset.

Altostratus: A thin, mid-level layer of grey cloud which is spread over a wide area. The sun is often faintly visible through it.

Altocumulus: These mid-level clouds appear as fluffy patches, which make the sky look as if it has a thin covering of wool.

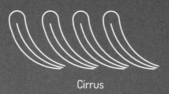

Cirrus

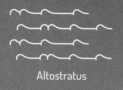

Altostratus

Cumulus

Altocumulus

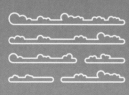

Stratus

Stratocumulus

Cumulonimbus: Thick and billowing, these are storm clouds. They usually have a flat base which is fairly close to ground level, but tower high up into the sky. They can be white or grey.

Cumulus: Fluffy, rounded, picture-perfect clouds – usually bright white and appearing on sunny days.

Stratocumulus: Low-level cloud that gives the sky a wide, patchy cover. Spots of blue sky are usually visible through the gaps.

Stratus: Long, flat, uniform, grey clouds that hang low in the sky, creating overcast days. They appear as fog or mist at ground level.

Veggie Kebabs

Makes 8-10 skewers

Not just for the barbecue, these veggie kebab skewers are rainbow-bright and nutrient-dense, whilst packing a real flavour punch.

Ingredients

2 courgettes

1 red onion

5 radishes

1 red and 1 yellow pepper

20 cherry tomatoes

20 mushrooms

Olive oil, to drizzle

Method

Lightly peel the courgettes, remove the stems, and cut into thick discs. Peel the onion, and cut into chunks. Wash, top and tail, and halve the radishes

De-stem and deseed the peppers, and cut into large chunks. Wash the tomatoes. Brush the mushrooms down with kitchen paper, then slice in half.

Arrange the vegetables on the skewers, making sure you have some of each kind per skewer, and varying the order. Brush or drizzle with olive oil, then cook on the barbecue, the grill, or in a griddle pan, until lightly charred.

Cottagecore inspiration

Make a Bug Hotel

Attract solitary bees and other insects into the garden with this simple bug hotel. This is a great way to repurpose items that you're likely to have to hand.

You will need

A large, empty food can

Can opener

Nail

Hammer

String

Bamboo canes – these must be hollow and can be of varying sizes

Secateurs

Instructions

Use a can opener to remove the bottom from an empty, clean can, leaving the centre tube. Place the base in the recycling. Make two small holes with your nail and hammer (big enough to thread string through) about halfway down the tin and about 5 cm (2 in.) apart.

Carefully push one end of the string into each of the holes and pull a small section through. Then knot each end and pull out the string so you have the means for hanging up your bug hotel.

Take a piece of bamboo and cut it with the secateurs into equal lengths that are a few centimetres longer than the can. Take another piece of bamboo and do the same again until you have enough canes so that when they are slotted into the can they are packed together tightly and don't move.

When it is finished, hang up your bug hotel so the can is on its side and the bamboo lies horizontally in the can. Be careful to pick a spot that gets some sunshine in the day but is sheltered from wind.

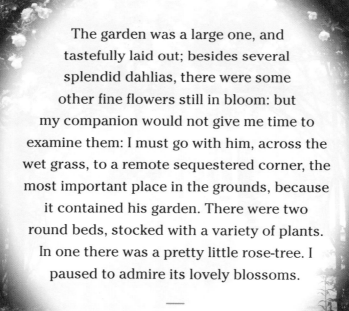

The garden was a large one, and tastefully laid out; besides several splendid dahlias, there were some other fine flowers still in bloom: but my companion would not give me time to examine them: I must go with him, across the wet grass, to a remote sequestered corner, the most important place in the grounds, because it contained his garden. There were two round beds, stocked with a variety of plants. In one there was a pretty little rose-tree. I paused to admire its lovely blossoms.

—

Anne Brontë, *Agnes Grey*

Branch hooks

If you're looking for extra hanging space but want something a bit different, try these branch hooks for size.

You will need

One branch per hook

Two screws per hook

Acrylic paint, optional

Paintbrush, if using paint

Saw

Drill

Instructions

Take off any excess limbs on your branch and cut the base at a right angle to make it easy to attach to the wall.

If you want to paint your branches, perhaps to match your décor, then do this now and allow to dry.

Drill two holes at the base of your branch, then add the screws to the holes and use the drill to drive these into the wall.

If you have painted your branches, dab some paint over the screws and allow to dry.

Your hooks are now ready to use.

Try to use windfall branches rather than sawing off tree branches, unless you're coppicing the tree purposefully.

If you place a bowl of water in the back of the oven, the steam it gives off will give your bread a crunchier crust.

No-Knead Ciabatta

Makes 2 ciabattas (or 2 ciabatte if you want to be authentic)

Beautiful, crusty ciabatta with no need to knead? Really? Yes, really, except you'll have to wait. The trick is to mix the ingredients together the day before you wish to eat it, as the dough requires 18 hours to rise.

Ingredients

500 g strong flour (your choice)

¼ tsp dried yeast

1½ tsp sea salt

470 ml lukewarm water

Method

Mix ingredients together in a mixing bowl and cover. Leave in a warm place for 18 hours.

Preheat oven to 200°C. Take your dough and place on a floured surface. Flatten slightly and fold the sides in to the centre. Gently pull the dough into two pieces and form into loose rectangular shapes – ciabatta literally translates from Italian as 'slipper'.

Bake on a tray on the floor of the oven for 30–35 minutes.

Why not chop a few olives and poke them into one of the doughs before baking? You can eat or share one of your ciabattas and freeze the other for another day. I also like to add 3 tbsp sourdough starter and 2 tbsp extra virgin olive oil, and use 60 ml less water, for flavour and digestive reasons.

Apple-Pie Milkshake

Serves 2 – multiply ingredients for more servings

**All the flavours of apple pie in a cool, milky drink?
Yes please!**

Ingredients

2 tart apples

25 g sugar

1½ tsp cinnamon

¾ tsp nutmeg

700 ml soya or oat milk

½ tsp vanilla extract

Maple syrup, to taste

Method

First, prepare your apples by peeling and chopping them. Add them to a saucepan with the sugar and one third of the cinnamon and nutmeg, to stew.

Shake together the non-dairy milk, remaining spices, vanilla extract and maple syrup, until the milk is frothy and the spices well distributed.

Divide between 2 glasses, and top with some of the stewed apple and a sprinkling of cinnamon.

For a thicker shake, blend the milk with 2 tablespoons of vanilla dairy-free ice cream, and some of the stewed apple – delicious!

Nettle Beer

Nettles can be found in abundance from early spring to late autumn. Gathering nettles can be painful if you're not dressed for it – opt for thick gardening gloves and keep your arms and legs covered. Your effort will be rewarded with this distinctive home brew.

Ingredients

1 large fabric grocery bag of nettle tops

5 l (8.8 pt) cold water

Irish moss (available online)

1 thumbnail-sized piece fresh root ginger, minced

500 g caster sugar

11.5 g packet of beer yeast

4 tbsp fresh lemon juice

Method

Give the nettle tops a shake to remove any bugs and rinse under the tap before placing in a large cooking pot with the cold water, Irish moss and ginger. Bring to the boil and simmer for 15 minutes.

Pour in the sugar and stir until dissolved. Once dissolved, take off the heat and allow to cool.

Activate the yeast, using the instructions on the packet, and add this to the mixture along with the lemon juice.

Cover the mixture and leave for three to four days to allow fermentation.

Decant into swing-top or screw-top bottles. Leave to chill in the fridge so it's ready to drink.

T-Shirt Quilt

This is a wonderful way to preserve your favourite T-shirts after they have passed their wear-by date. T-shirt fabric is the softest and cosiest and is perfect for snuggling. It makes a quilt of approximately 135 x 200 cm (53 x 78 in.).

Materials

10 T-shirts for a full-size quilt (using the front and back of each T-shirt), which will fit a single bed

Iron and ironing board

Cotton

Scissors

Sewing machine (or needle, thread and extreme patience!)

Tape measure

30 x 30 cm (11.8 x 11.8 in.) piece of cardboard for your patchwork template

Pins

Iron-on interfacing

Fabric for the backing of your quilt – use an old single sheet if you have one

Fire-retardant quilt batting (the soft stuff that acts as the filling in the sandwich between the front and the back of the quilt) – the eco-friendliest is made from bamboo. All are readily available from craft stores or online

Bias binding for the edge of the quilt

Give your T-shirts an iron and then cut each along the edge, and remove the neck and cuffs so that you have two large pieces of fabric from each T-shirt.

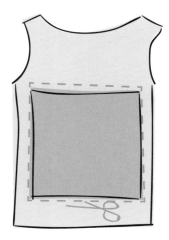

Cut the squares from your T-shirts, using your patchwork template as a guide. If there are patterns or words on the T-shirts, take a bit of time to work out which part of the design you want on show. Cut interfacing to the same size as the template and then iron on the interfacing to each T-shirt square – this is not essential but it does make the fabric easier to sew as stretchy material can be difficult to work with.

When all the pieces have been cut out, lay them out on a clean floor to determine where each piece will go – see which designs and colours work best together. For this pattern we are working on the premise of five rows of four squares.

When you're happy with your design, it's time to begin sewing. First, take two T-shirt squares that will be next to each other. Put one on top of the other, with the right sides facing inwards. Pin them in place, then sew along the edge 5 mm (0.2 in.) in. This half centimetre is for selvedge.

Continue sewing the squares together in this way. For ease, sew separate rows together first, and then sew the rows together to form the quilt (rather than making the whole quilt straight away).

When the T-shirt pieces are all sewn together, give it an iron and turn over to tie up loose threads. Measure it to check how short or oversized it is compared to the average single quilt, which is approximately 135 x 200 cm (53 x 78 in.). Remember, you can make it any size you wish!

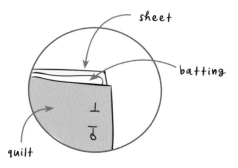

sheet

batting

quilt

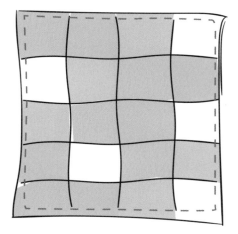

Cut the batting and old sheet to approximately 135 x 200 cm (53 x 78 in.) and pin everything together (right sides facing out) – sheet on the bottom, batting in the middle and quilt on top. Sew pieces together. For a more 'quilty' effect, sew along the lines of the edges of each T-shirt square.

Remember to tie loose ends and trim edges for your sewing as you go along to avoid getting threads in a tangle.

Next you will need some bias binding which will cover the raw edges and give your quilt a professional finish. Look online for ways to make your own bias binding out of oddments of fabric, or purchase some from haberdashers or craft stores.

Begin by cutting four lengths of bias binding that are slightly longer than your quilt edges – make sure you have 2.5 cm (1 in.) excess bias at each edge. Then unfold the bias binding and pin the right side of the binding against the front of your quilt, aligning the edge against the raw edge of the quilt. Pin into place.

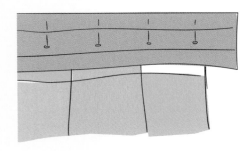

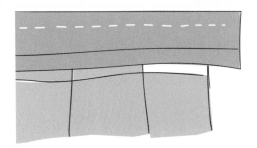

Now sew along the first crease, making sure to catch the front and back of the quilt.

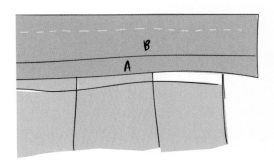

Next, fold up flap A. Then fold flap B up so it's flat against the quilt, and turn the whole thing over so the back of the quilt is facing you.

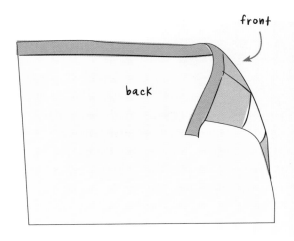

Fold the binding over to the back of the quilt so you have equal widths of bias on the front and back, then iron for a neat crease. Turn the quilt over again and pin the front and back of the binding into place. Sew a running stitch a couple of millimetres from the edge of the binding for a neat finish with the top of the quilt facing you.

There are a couple of options for finishing bias binding edges. If you're feeling adventurous, look online for tutorials on making mitred corners. However, the simplest way is to square off the ends and tuck in a small amount to avoid fraying. To do this, make sure the back of the quilt is facing you. Take one end of binding and fold up section A. Then fold section B so the binding is flat against the back of the quilt and pin in place. Turn the quilt over and sew running stitch a couple of millimetres from the edge of the binding for a neat finish. Repeat for all the loose ends of binding.

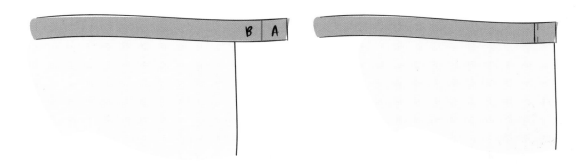

Autumn

The nights are drawing in and while temperatures may be dropping, this transitional season offers a plethora of cosy activities. Autumn brings with it a beautiful palette of rich, earthy tones that evoke a sense of warmth and contentment – paradigms of the cottagecore aesthetic.

The following tips will help you create the ultimate homely haven with advice on how to store firewood, create bath bombs and make hearty homemade soup. Read on to learn how to let the glorious colours of autumn permeate your spaces and how best to enjoy this humble season.

Introduce Nature into Your Home

Nature acts like a healing balm for our body and mind, and creates a relaxing, welcoming environment. As the days start to get cooler, you can start to bring nature inside so you can enjoy it year-round. Houseplants and fresh-cut flowers are the obvious place to start. They brighten up any space and fill the air with glorious scents. For a natural look, pick a few flowers from your garden and place them into jam jars; collect pretty pebbles, shells and driftwood; and make table decorations out of bark, leaves, berries and pine cones – things that you have found on a country or seaside walk. Introduce warm, organic textures to your home with natural wood flooring and furniture, hand-thrown pottery and pebbles. Natural materials are an easy way to make your home look beautiful and connected to the outdoors.

Rag rug

Making a rag rug is a wonderful way of using up old fabric, such as towels, sheets and clothing. T-shirts and towels make the softest rag rugs, but there is something special about using old clothes worn by you and/or family members that perhaps no longer fit or are beyond repair: you're literally weaving memories into the rug, which you can be reminded of every time you use it. It also serves as a homely way to reduce draughts on bare floorboards.

You will need

Old fabric

Canvas with 1 cm grid width, cut to the size that you want for your rag rug

Fabric scissors

Nimble fingers (!)

Instructions

Use the fabric scissors to snip the edge of the fabric at 5 cm intervals to make it easier to tear. Then tear the fabric into strips.

Think about the colour combinations of the rug before you start. You could use dye if you have a particular colour or effect in mind, or simply go freestyle and opt for the multicoloured look.

Take your first strip and push it into the first grid square and out so that the edge of the canvas square is in the middle of the strip.

Make a double overhand knot with the fabric strip and pull tight. Then take another strip and push this into the next hole and do the same process until you have your rug!

The great thing about these rag rugs is that they can be washed in the machine as if you were still washing the clothes that they're made of. It's also a craft that doesn't require your undivided attention so you can do it while watching your favourite soap.

Woodland Walks

To reconnect with the simple things in life, wrap up, don your walking boots and head to the woods. Trees provide shelter for all sorts of animals, so woods are fantastic places to look and listen for wildlife. Perhaps you'll hear the call of a cuckoo or owl, or see the tracks of a fox or badger. Maybe you'll find shiny conkers scattered beneath the branches of a horse chestnut tree in autumn. Woods are exciting places to explore. You can turn the walk into a scavenger hunt – there are so many things to pick up and collect, such as pine cones, leaves, acorns and feathers. Tap into your playful side by hugging a tree or balancing on logs. Being in the woods is a great way to recharge your batteries. Trees emit aromatics and chemicals which enhance our well-being and encourage us to relax. Head to the woods and soak up the revitalizing atmosphere.

Fruit Crumble

Serves 4

Home-made fruit crumble is the ultimate comfort food and is guaranteed to keep the cold at bay. This cinnamon-infused apple and blackberry crumble has a rich, golden oaty topping for a satisfying crunch. Serve it with ice cream or lashings of custard.

Ingredients

5 apples, peeled and
   cut into cubes

150 g blackberries

6 tbsp light-brown
   soft sugar

½ tsp cinnamon

1 tsp vanilla extract

For the topping

100 g plain flour

2 tbsp brown sugar

¼ tsp cinnamon

50 g unsalted butter,
   chilled and cubed

4 tbsp oats

Method

Preheat the oven to 180°C/350°F/Gas 4.

Place the chopped apples with the blackberries, sugar, cinnamon and vanilla extract in a heavy bottomed pot. Mix well and cook for 5 minutes over a medium heat.

Meanwhile, make the topping by mixing the flour, sugar and cinnamon in a small bowl. Rub the butter into the mix until it resembles breadcrumbs, then mix in the oats.

Spoon the fruit mixture into the ovenproof dish and sprinkle the crumble on top. Bake for 15–20 minutes until golden and bubbling.

Stacking and Storing Firewood

If you're the proud owner of an open fire or wood-burning stove, you'll know how important it is to make sure you have enough logs to see you through the winter chill. Sitting in front of a crackling fire is the epitome of cosy cottage life. But did you know that in order for your fire to burn efficiently, you need to stack your firewood properly?

First, buy logs which have been cut into short lengths (ideally 25 cm long) and split them to speed up drying. Then store your logs in a well-ventilated log store. A common error is to pile the logs on the ground and cover them with tarpaulin, but this encourages mould and decay to spread. Air circulation is one of the most important factors in keeping your firewood dry and investing in a log store will pay dividends, as it allows the wood to be stacked off the ground. It should have a roof over the top and the sides should be open to the air.

Position your log store on a sheltered side of the house. To encourage air circulation, stack your wood in rows, leaving gaps between the rows. If stacking against a wall or fence, leave about 10 cm between the logs and the surface.

Well-stacked wood looks attractive but, crucially, it will be nice and dry by the time you need it. Dry wood burns efficiently and gives off less smoke. A warm, cosy household is never short of dry firewood!

An Evening Off-Grid

There's magic to be had in slowing down your evenings, from telling ghost stories to having a cheese and wine night. Here are some ideas for cosy nights in, whether you live alone or with family or friends.

Games night

Get your brain working on problem-solving and strategy with a board or card game. And who says you need to stick to the official rules? Make up your own – a round of hide-and-seek between games, allowing slang and text language in a game of Scrabble or homemade cookies (see page 97) for the winner.

IT'S MOVIE TIME

Film night

Light the fire, get out your favourite blanket and snuggle on the sofa with a bowl of popcorn. Try making food that matches what you're watching – fondue or hotpot for a film set in snow, mocktails for a film set on a desert island, for example. And why not embrace your inner child and make a den out of cushions and blankets for the ultimate cosy movie experience?

Book club

Settle in for a long comfy night with a good book – the ultimate self-care evening as the nights draw in. The best stories challenge your perceptions, shape you and become part of you, but sometimes the best book is the one you've read a million times and that makes you happy every time. If you're not a huge reader, try starting with the classics – *Little Women*, *The Secret Garden*, *The Lord of the Rings* or some Jane Austen.

Cottagecore inspiration

Bath Bombs

The excitement of watching the fizz of a bath bomb never gets old. Here's the eco-thrifty way to get your fix.

Makes 1 bomb

Ingredients

60 g bicarbonate of soda

30 g Epsom salts

30 g cornflour

30 g citric acid

3 tsp olive oil (any type is fine)

1 tbsp natural essential oils (you could use a mix of your favourites)

1 tsp natural food colouring

1 tbsp tap water

Bath bomb mould

Instructions

Place all the dry ingredients in a bowl and mix thoroughly with a metal spoon.

Pour the citric acid, olive oil, essential oils, food colouring and water into a jug and mix well.

Slowly pour the wet ingredients into the bowl with the dry ingredients and mix as you go. The mixture should be the consistency of wet sand.

Scoop the mixture into your mould, seal and leave to harden for a couple of hours.

When the bomb has set, it's ready for the bath. Or you can wrap the bath bombs in tissue paper or fabric scraps and keep them or gift them. They'll last for 12 months.

Lighting Candles

There's a reason why Danes burn more candles per person than anywhere else in Europe – sharing cosy moments is important when braving the leaden skies and harsh Scandinavian winters, and lighting candles is one of the quickest ways of creating a warm and inviting atmosphere. Place candles, tea lights and lanterns around your home – on the dinner table, surrounding the fireplace and next to your computer – the more twinkly the better! Make sure you position your candles carefully as anything that brings fire into your home can be dangerous. Here is a list of dos and don'ts to keep you safe:

Do

- Always put candles on a heat-resistant surface. Be especially careful with tea lights as they can become hot enough to melt plastic.

- Place candles in a proper holder so they are held upright and won't fall over.

- Position candles well away from curtains, fabrics and any overhanging objects, and keep them out of strong draughts.

- Make sure your candles are out of reach of children and pets.

- Take special care with scented candles as they turn to liquid to release their fragrance. Put them on a glass or metal holder.

- Candles that have been put out can go on smouldering for some time. Double-check that they are completely extinguished.

Don't

- Don't place a candle under a shelf as it can easily burn the surface.

- Never lean over a candle as clothing and hair can easily catch light.

- Don't leave candles burning if you leave the room.

- Avoid moving a burning candle – always snuff out the flame first.

- Never leave a burning candle or oil burner in a child's bedroom or go to sleep with a candle burning.

- When extinguishing a candle, don't blow it out as this can send sparks and hot wax flying. Use a snuffer or a spoon to put them out.

Pom-pom for a Beanie

Upcycle one of your tired woolly beanies with a bit of winter cheer! Pom-poms are great fun to make – and why stop with one pom-pom when you could have ten, in different colours?

What you'll need

Cardboard

Scissors

Yarn

Needle and thread

Instructions

1

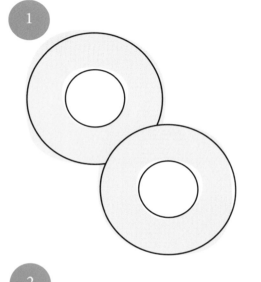

Cut out two cardboard discs of the same size (the bigger the disc, the bigger the pom-pom).

Cut a small hole in the middle of each disc and lay them on top of each other. Make sure the hole is big enough to pass the yarn through.

2

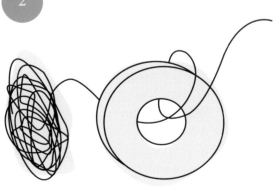

Loop the yarn through the holes and around the outer edges of the discs, holding it in place with your fingers to begin with to make sure it does not unravel.

3

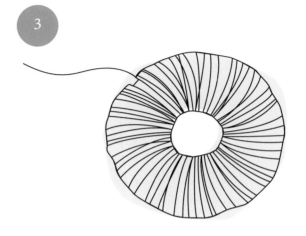

Repeat until the discs are completely and evenly covered.

4

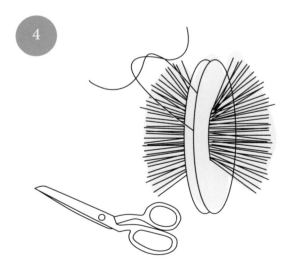

Place the scissors between the two discs of cardboard and cut through the yarn that's around the outer edge.

Carefully wrap a long piece of thread between each disc around the yarn that's between the two discs and tie a knot to hold your pom-pom together. (Leave enough thread to sew the pom-pom onto your hat.)

5

Once the yarn is securely tied, cut the cardboard and pull it away from the pom-pom.

Fluff up your pom-pom and give it a trim with scissors, if necessary, to make it perfectly round.

Sew the pom-pom onto your hat and go out into the crisp, cold air with a jaunty spring in your step.

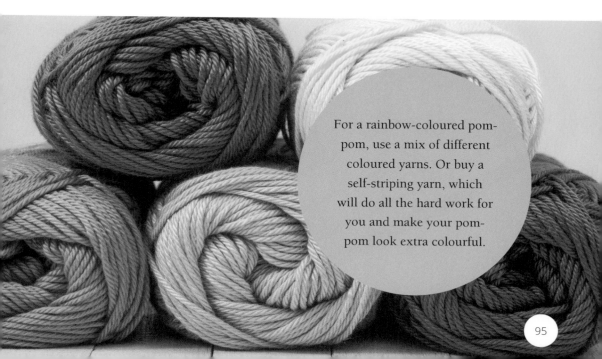

For a rainbow-coloured pom-pom, use a mix of different coloured yarns. Or buy a self-striping yarn, which will do all the hard work for you and make your pom-pom look extra colourful.

Choc Chip Cookies

Makes 6 large cookies

Who'd have thought it – cookies made from pulses? These tasty treats give you all the proteiny goodness of chickpeas and will satisfy your craving for something sweet at the same time.

Ingredients

1 x 400 g can chickpeas, drained and rinsed

2 tbsp peanut butter

1 tbsp maple syrup

2 tsp vanilla extract

1 tsp baking powder

75 g cocoa nibs or chocolate chips

Method

Preheat the oven to 180°C and grease a baking tray (or line a silicon mat with baking parchment).

Blitz the chickpeas in a blender until smooth; then add in the peanut butter, maple syrup, vanilla extract and baking powder. Blend again until smooth and creamy.

Stir through the cocoa nibs or chocolate chips.

Divide the dough into 6 pieces, roll into balls and then press them down gently on the baking tray.

Bake for 15 minutes, until golden. Remove from the oven and rest for 5 minutes. Move to a wire rack to cool and see how long you can wait before trying one!

These taste lovely served warm with a little coconut ice-cream. You can even eat the cookie mixture without cooking it – no eggs, so no need to worry – but if you're doing this, leave out the baking powder and chill the dough in the fridge first.

Digging

Today I think
Only with scents – scents dead leaves yield,
And bracken, and wild carrot's seed,
And the square mustard field;

Odours that rise
When the spade wounds the root of tree,
Rose, currant, raspberry, or goutweed,
Rhubarb or celery;

The smoke's smell, too,
Flowing from where a bonfire burns
The dead, the waste, the dangerous,
And all to sweetness turns.

It is enough
To smell, to crumble the dark earth,
While the robin sings over again
Sad songs of Autumn mirth.

Edward Thomas

Butternut Squash Soup

Welcome yourself home with a big bowl of creamy butternut squash soup. Easy to make and very nutritious, this dinner-time treat is the equivalent of a cosy knitted jumper (plus you can reheat it for lunch!).

Ingredients

1 large or 2 small
butternut squashes

Handful of fresh,
chopped sage leaves

Freshly ground
black pepper

1–2 tbsp olive oil

2 onions, chopped

1 litre chicken or
vegetable stock

To serve (optional)

Crème fraîche

Pumpkin seeds

A sprinkle of fresh
thyme leaves

A sliver of blue cheese

Salt and pepper

Method

Preheat the oven to 180°C/350°F/Gas 4.

Deseed the butternut squash (no need to peel it) and cut into large cubes. Mix with the sage leaves, black pepper and olive oil. Tip the mixture into a roasting tin and bake in the oven for around 35–45 minutes.

While the squash is cooking, sauté the onions in a large saucepan until translucent. When the butternut squash has softened and the sage leaves are crispy, add the mix to the onions and cover with the stock.

Simmer for 30 minutes, then remove from the heat, season to taste and blend using a hand-blender until smooth (for a really silky soup, liquidize in a blender).

Decorate with fresh thyme leaves and pumpkin seeds on top of swirls of crème fraîche and a sliver of blue cheese. Add salt and pepper to taste. Serve with crusty bread.

Fruit Picking in the Hedgerows

Autumn hedgerows are bursting with delicious edible treasure; fruits such as sloes, blackberries and elderberries are just asking to be picked. So grab a bag or a basket and harvest the wild hedgerows. Foraging is a great way to reconnect with nature while enjoying the last of the fine weather. Pluck blackberries from bushes to make a fruit crumble, pick bunches of ripe elderberries for a delicious sweet jelly or collect sloes to make gin. Make sure you take a guidebook or expert with you so you know what's safe to eat, and *never* eat anything you're unsure of.

Berry Jam

Cottagecore is all about doing little things that make you happy, such as making home-made jam. After an hour in the kitchen immersed in stirring, bottling and labelling, the berries are transformed into jars of fruity loveliness, ready to be slathered onto hot, buttered toast or a scone. Sticky and sweet, this jam will give you a warm glow of satisfaction that comes from making something with your own fair hands.

Ingredients

500 g mixed seasonal berries, such as blackberries, loganberries and raspberries

300 g sugar

1.5 tbsp lemon juice

Method

Place the berries in a large saucepan, bring slowly to boiling point and then simmer for 5 minutes.

Add in the sugar, stir and leave to simmer for 10–15 minutes. Remove the pan from the heat and stir in the lemon juice.

Pour the jam into sterilized jars and seal with a lid. Leave to set and cool.

The jam will keep for at least a year if stored in a cool, dry cupboard, but once opened it must be stored in a fridge.

Create a Nature Display

Do you always come back from a walk with your pockets full of unusual stones, twigs and leaves? If you're stumped for what to do with your finds when you get back home, try making a nature display. It's great fun sorting through your findings and thinking of fun ways to display them. You could arrange a collection of shells and driftwood from the beach or place interesting rocks and pebbles in glass jars. Berry branches and pine cones look striking when arranged in large vases or can be hung from the ceiling like a giant mobile. Don't limit your display to a table in the corner. Experiment by arranging your treasures in a tray or a box, or make a feature of them on a mantelpiece or shelf. This is a great way to reconnect with the wonder of nature, and the beauty of it is that the whole family can get involved. Happy collecting!

Things to collect

Woodland and countryside:
Moss, pine cones, hazelnuts, twigs, fallen tree bark, conkers, field maple or sycamore helicopters and acorns

Garden:
Dried sunflower heads, seed pods, dandelion clocks, stones, leaves, petals, squashes and gourds

Beach:
Shells (without creatures inside), whelk egg cases, dried seaweed, seagull feathers, mermaid's purses and sharks' teeth

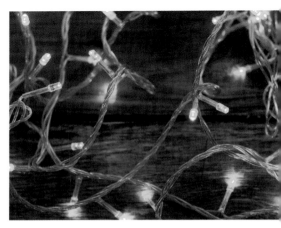

Winter

Winter calls for a safe sanctuary of peace and calm, so take inspiration from our hibernating animal friends and find solace in your living space this winter, complete with log fire and roasted chestnuts. The following pages will help lift your spirits, perhaps by encouraging you to indulge in a dish of hearty ribollita – or perhaps a cinnamon hot chocolate is more your speed?

Nature still has a great amount to offer in these darker months, so be sure to take the opportunity to breathe in the fresh, cool air and delight in the wonder of winter.

A Breath of
Fresh Air

In winter you may not get as many opportunities to get out in nature, so bring greenery into your home instead. Many houseplants are amazing purifiers for indoor environments. They cleanse the air in your home by filtering out harmful toxins and pollutants. According to a NASA study, the following plants are the best air-filtering ones to buy (NASA recommends having at least one plant per 100 square feet of home or office space):

- *Aloe vera*
- Bamboo palm (*Dypsis lutescens*)
- Banana palm (*Musa basjoo*)
- Barberton daisy (*Gerbera jamesonii*)
- Boston fern (*Nephrolepis exaltata*)
- Broadleaf lady palm (*Rhapis excelsa*)
- Chinese evergreen (*Aglaonema*)
- Devil's ivy (*Epipremnum aureum*)
- Dumb cane (*Dieffenbachia*)
- Elephant ear philodendron (*Philodendron domesticum*)
- English ivy (*Hedera helix*)
- Flamingo lily (*Anthurium andraeanum*)
- Florist's daisy (*Chrysanthemum morifolium*)
- Heart-leaf philodendron (*Philodendron cordatum*)
- Kimberly queen fern (*Nephrolepis obliterata*)
- Lily turf (*Liriope muscari*)
- Moth orchids (*Phalaenopsis*)
- Peace lily (*Spathiphyllum*)

Open Fires

Relaxing in front of a log fire is one of life's great pleasures. A log fire, be it an open hearth or a modern wood burner, creates a warm, cosy atmosphere with its crackles and flickering flames. The comforting aroma of wood smoke calms and soothes, evoking primal connection and a sense of belonging. The fireplace is the meeting point and the warm heart of the home, the place where stories are shared and celebrations are toasted. Welcome family and friends to gather at the fireside and enjoy simple pleasures, such as cooking marshmallows or playing board games, or lose yourself in the reverie of watching the flames dance.

A hearth of one's own is worth gold.

Danish proverb

Whittling and Carving

One of the wonderful aspects of cottagecore life is developing an affinity for nature, so you can create things you need using its bountiful resources with skills such as whittling (carving and shaving layers off branches and sticks). With your own two hands, you can make all manner of things come into being: cups, spoons, fire starters and even tent pegs.

You will need a knife for all of the following. There is a variety to choose from, including penknives and folding knives, but a fixed-blade knife (with a protective sheath for when it's not in use) is possibly the safest to use, as there's no risk of the blade folding back on itself. You can find whittling-specific knives at outdoor stores and online.

Marshmallow stick

Similar to the above, find a dry, moss-free stick from the surrounding area that's roughly the width of a pencil and approximately 50 centimetres long. Use your knife to take shavings off the tip of the stick, working your way round until you have a sharp point. Then shave off the outer bark to about 15 centimetres above the pointy end. Make sure there are no splinters, and your stick is ready for a session of marshmallow toasting.

Shavings

Making shavings is a good way to practise your whittling skills to start off with, and the shavings make great kindling for a campfire. Find a dry stick (already on the ground) and run your knife blade away from yourself down the edge of the stick, slowly and at a slight angle, shaving off small sections.

Feather stick

Once you've mastered the art of making shavings, try a feather stick. Do just as you would do with normal shavings, but stop your knife just before the shaving becomes detached, so you create a curl or 'feather'. Continue doing this on one side of the stick until you have something that resembles a feather duster. These make great tinder if dry grass is in short supply.

Tent peg

If you want to make something a little bigger, try carving a tent peg. For this you will need a camping or folding saw in addition to your knife. Begin by searching for thick sticks approximately 20 centimetres long and 3 centimetres in diameter. Use your knife to sharpen one end into a point. Then measure approximately 5 centimetres down from the unsharpened end and use your saw to cut roughly a quarter of the way through the stick. Switch to your knife and make another cut at a 45-degree angle to the saw mark. This is the notch that the tent rope will sit in. Finally, use the knife to round off the top of the peg, as this will stop the peg splitting when you hammer it into the ground.

Cottagecore inspiration

Shampoo Bars

Shampoo in a bar! These luxurious bars are brilliant for reducing your plastic consumption and saving money. They are simple to make too – make up a batch for yourself and your friends. They're also highly portable – if you're going on holiday, you won't find a puddle of gunge at the bottom of your bag as there is nothing to spill and they can be taken on board aircraft in your hand luggage.

Makes two standard-sized shampoo bars

Ingredients

125 g Castile melt and pour soap base (available at chemists and online)

1½ tsp argan oil

½ tsp black treacle

10 drops lavender essential oil

10 drops rose essential oil

10 drops jasmine essential oil

Pure alcohol spray

Equipment

Saucepan

Metal or heatproof mixing bowl that fits neatly over your saucepan

Sharp knife

Metal spoon

Dropper

Silicone soap moulds – available from craft suppliers online

Instructions

Begin by cutting your Castile melt and pour soap base into 1 cm (0.4 in.) cubes and placing them in the metal or heatproof bowl.

Fill the saucepan with water so that when you place the metal bowl over the pan the water is just grazing the bowl. Heat the water on a medium heat.

As the contents of the bowl begin to melt, stir the liquid with a metal spoon until it has melted and is a runny consistency – this is your shampoo base.

Once the shampoo base has melted, mix in the argan oil and black treacle.

Remove your shampoo mixture from the heat and allow to cool for five minutes.

Using a dropper, add in the essential oils and mix with the spoon.

Pour the shampoo mixture into your moulds and leave to set overnight.

Once the shampoo is solid, turn it out and slice into palm-sized chunks with a sharp knife.

It's now ready to use and will keep for six months.

Many soap or shampoo bar recipes contain a substance called lye, which can cause breathing difficulties if not handled correctly. This recipe does not contain lye. The essential oils are just a suggestion – choose your own favourite aromas!

Cinnamon Hot Chocolate

Serves 1

This sumptuous hot chocolate recipe is a warming hug in a mug.

Ingredients

1 tbsp cocoa powder

1 tbsp sugar

¼ tsp ground cinnamon

½ tsp vanilla extract

2 tbsp and 180 ml
   milk (dairy or nut)

To serve (optional)

Cream

Marshmallows

Cinnamon

Method

Mix together the cocoa powder, sugar, cinnamon, vanilla and 2 tbsp of milk in a mug. Use a fork or a mini whisk until the mixture resembles a thick syrup.

Over a medium heat, warm the rest of the milk until it begins to bubble, then pour it into the mug with the chocolate syrup and stir thoroughly.

For added indulgence, serve with a dollop of cream or marshmallows and a sprinkle of cinnamon.

Mug Cosy

Make your favourite mug a smart
little jacket for winter – not only
will it look very fetching but it
will keep your hot chocolate
steaming that little bit longer.
It's also a genius way to upcycle
a woolly sock!

What you'll need

Mug

Ruler

Woolly sock

Scissors

Needle and thread

Fabric glue (optional)

Optional extras: buttons, felt shapes,
mini pom-poms, sequins

Instructions

1

Choose your favourite mug and measure its height.

2

Cut the sock at the ankle and keep the top section.

Turn the top section of the sock inside out and hem the seams securely with the thread.

3

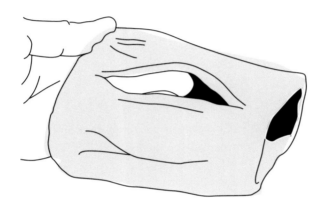

Turn the sock the right side out and carefully cut a slit for the mug handle. Overstitch the edges or use the fabric glue to prevent fraying. If using glue, be sparing so it will dry clear, and leave to dry for the time it suggests on the packet. Then fit your cosy over the mug.

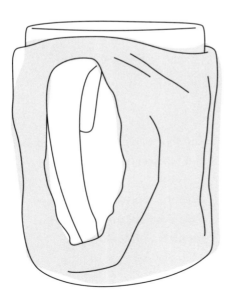

Winter Slow-Cooker Ribollita

Serves 6

Preparation time

10 minutes

Cooking time

8 hours, 45 minutes

Ingredients

2 medium onions

200 g carrot

300 g celery

1 fennel bulb

4 cloves garlic

2 bay leaves

1 kg ham hock

400 g tin chopped tomatoes

3 sprigs fresh rosemary

1 tsp dried chilli flakes

2 litres vegetable stock

350 g curly kale

400 g tin cannellini beans

250 g slightly stale country-style or sourdough bread

40 g Parmesan cheese

Method

Chop one onion and the carrot finely, slice the celery and fennel thinly and quarter the remaining onion. Crush the garlic. Add these ingredients to the slow cooker with the bay leaves, ham hock, tin of tomatoes (undrained), rosemary, chilli and vegetable stock. Cook on low for 8 hours.

Remove the ham from the cooker and set aside to cool. Add the curly kale and cannellini beans. Cook on high until the kale is completely wilted.

When the ham is comfortable to touch, shred the meat from the bone. Don't use the fat, skin or bone. (You can make ham stock for the future if you have any spare onion, celery and carrot leftover. Chop them finely, combine with the bone and cover with water. Simmer on low for 40 minutes and strain.)

Add the meat back into the slow cooker and season to taste.

Tear the bread into chunks and add a handful to each bowl. Cover with the soup and grate the Parmesan over it.

This traditional Italian peasant's dish makes the most of winter vegetables, larder essentials and leftover bread. It makes plenty and any remainders can be reheated – *ribollita* is 'reboiled' in Italian – over the following days to make a hearty lunch. Onion, carrot and fennel should be at their best in the winter season and available at your local fresh produce supplier. Rosemary and bay add real depth of flavour; winter is the perfect time to utilize these sturdy herb-garden favourites as they will be unruffled by the cold. Set the cooker to start in the morning and you will be welcomed in from the dark evening by a delicious scent.

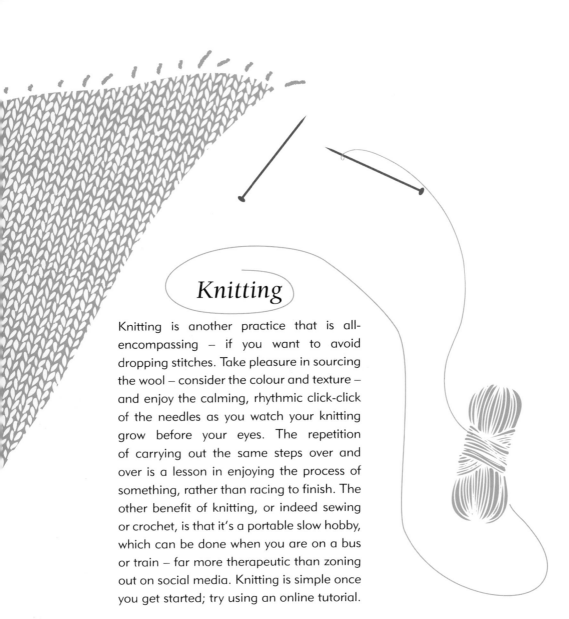

Knitting

Knitting is another practice that is all-encompassing – if you want to avoid dropping stitches. Take pleasure in sourcing the wool – consider the colour and texture – and enjoy the calming, rhythmic click-click of the needles as you watch your knitting grow before your eyes. The repetition of carrying out the same steps over and over is a lesson in enjoying the process of something, rather than racing to finish. The other benefit of knitting, or indeed sewing or crochet, is that it's a portable slow hobby, which can be done when you are on a bus or train – far more therapeutic than zoning out on social media. Knitting is simple once you get started; try using an online tutorial.

Make Do and Mend

Here are some basic skills that only require a simple sewing kit.

Sew a button

You will need

Replacement button

Needle and thread

Scissors

Method

Start by looking closely at where the button was originally positioned. It's usually fairly easy as there will be strands of thread and pinpricks from the stitches.

Thread your needle and tie a knot to the end. Stitch from the inside of the garment to the front and secure the thread with one or two stitches, so you're not just relying on the strength of the knot to eventually hold the button.

Thread the needle through the button and begin to stitch the buttonholes. For a two-button hole, stitch up through one hole and down the other. For four holes, repeat the stitching so you have two parallel stitches.

When you have a good amount of stitches (around five to ten), take the thread underneath the button and wind it round the stitches a few times before sewing some stitches to the underside of the fabric to secure the stitching in place. Then trim the excess cotton.

Patch It

Patches have come a long way since leather or cloth patches were used to cover up threadbare elbows in jackets. There is an abundance of patches available, including hand-embroidered bees, retro Scout and Guide badges, tattoo styles and everything else you can think of, so when you've got a hole forming in your clothes that is simply too big to darn, there's no need for your heart to sink – see it as an opportunity to get creative!

You will need

A patch

Pins

A large needle

Yarn

Sewing scissors

Method

Position the patch and hold it in place with pins. Take your needle and thread a length of yarn onto it, then tie a knot to the end.

Thread the needle from the back of the fabric and through the edge of the patch.

Overstitch around the edge of the patch using small stitches.

Finish off by winding the needle back through a few stitches, pushing the needle through to the back of the fabric and sewing some tiny stitches to an area of undamaged fabric underneath the patch.

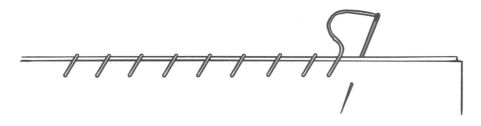

Darn It

Make holes vanish the traditional way! Darning is an art that may take a little time to master but it'll save you money and heartache when your favourite top has been chomped by moths.

You will need

Darning mushroom

A large needle

Yarn – either matching your item or contrasting if you want to make a feature of it

Sewing scissors

Method

Place the mushroom under the hole. Sew a couple of stitches about 5 mm (0.2 in.) from the hole then sew over those stitches to secure the thread.

Sew small running stitches around the perimeter of the hole, around 5 mm (0.2 in.) from the edge.

Stitch horizontally across the hole from one edge of the running stitches to the other.

Then carefully weave over and under the horizontal stitches vertically (see pictures).

When you have finished, secure with three stitches on top of each other on the perimeter of the circle that you originally sewed. Cut and neaten.

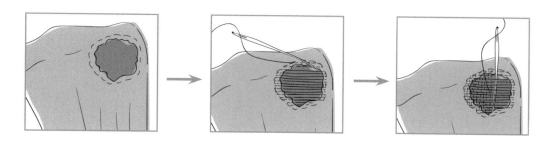

Felt Slippers

Slippers are essential attire for pyjama days. No slippers? No problem! Show your feet some love with these felt slippers, which will keep you feeling toasty all year round.

What you'll need

Paper

50 x 50 cm square of wool felt

Scissors

Dressmaker's chalk or fabric marker

Strong thread, such as silk or polyester

Large darning needle

Instructions

1 Enlarge and cut out the template below so that it is twice as wide and a couple of centimetres longer than the sole of your shoe – either scan it and print it or enlarge it on a photocopier.

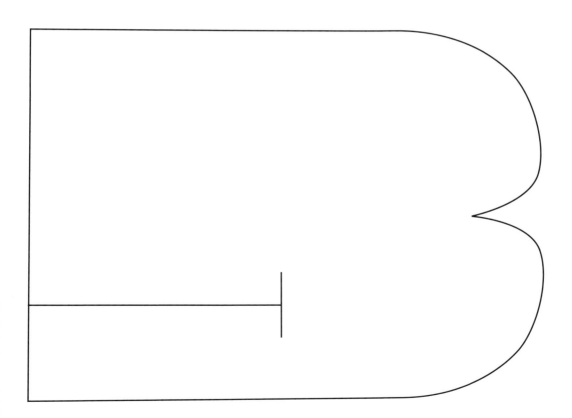

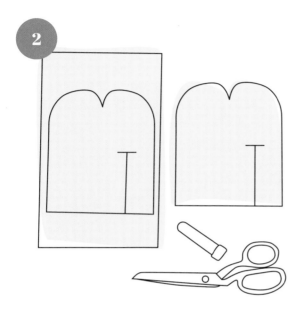

2

Trace the template onto your felt and cut carefully, including the 'T' shape.

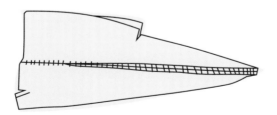

3

Fold the felt in half lengthways, and stitch the seam of the toe. Pinch the heel seams together and sew from the top of the slipper to approximately 2 cm from the heel and carefully snip into the heel to create a small flap.

4

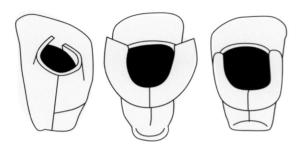

Tuck this flap in and sew it securely. Then, turn the slipper inside out and tidy the edges of the flap by rounding them with your scissors.

You can either finish there or fold the sides down to the ankle and sew these against the slipper.

When sewing the other slipper, remember to flip the template so the 'T' is on the opposite side.

Try customizing your slippers with home-made felt flowers for extra cuteness!

Roasted Chestnuts

Serves 4-6

Roasted chestnuts are the perfect excuse to cuddle up with your loved ones by the fire. Cooked to perfection, their pale insides become nutty, creamy and surprisingly sweet. Serve as they are or dip them in spiced melted butter.

Ingredients

1 kg chestnuts

For the spiced butter

60 g unsalted butter

1 cinnamon stick

Pinch of nutmeg, salt
    and sugar

For the spiced butter

Melt the butter over a low heat and stir in the spices, salt and sugar. Once melted, remove the cinnamon stick and transfer the mixture to a small dish for dipping.

Method

Heat the oven to 200°C/400°F/Gas 6.

Lay the chestnuts on their flat sides and use a sharp knife to cut a long slit or a cross in the curved shell (when you roast them, the steam will escape and they won't explode).

Place in a roasting tin in a single layer, flat side down, and bake until the skin splits open. This should take around 30 minutes.

When the chestnuts are cool enough to handle, peel away the tough outer skin and pop the sweet white kernel into your mouth.

To bake on a fire

Place the prepared chestnuts in a cast-iron frying pan or a skillet in a single layer.

Position the pan in the glowing embers of the fire.

Turn the chestnuts over from time to time so they cook evenly. They will take 5–10 minutes to cook.

Repair, Restore, Upcycle

Before purchasing new, think of all the old furniture out there, the preloved tables and chairs that find their way to second-hand stores and online auction sites – you could even call it 'vintage' to make it sound more appealing! There are many outlets that sell second-hand furniture nowadays, and with a bit of creative flair you can adapt your finds into something unique and truly special. Here are some ideas to whet your appetite for upcycling furniture.

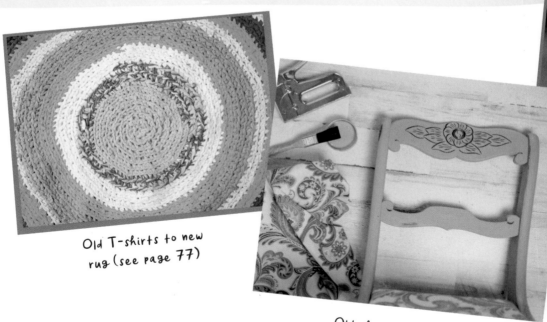

Old T-shirts to new rug (see page 77)

Old chair + sample paint pot + fabric offcut = new chair!

Copper pipes to
candlesticks or
plant holders

Mirror frames to
picture frames

Lab stools to plant stands

139

Sourdough

The slow-rising quality of sourdough breads is favoured by many for being easier to digest and for its superior flavour. Sourdough is bread made without adding yeast – 'wild yeast' and lactic acid bacteria present in flour allow it to naturally ferment, if given time, into a wonderful, ripe, living 'starter'. During the bread-making process, the starter ferments the sugars in the dough, helping the bread rise and acquire its characteristic taste. Lactic acid bacteria are present in other fermented foods such as kimchi, yoghurt, kefir, pickles and sauerkraut.

FOR YOUR STARTER
Ingredients

1 kg packet any wholemeal, stoneground flour, such as rye, spelt or wheat

Water

Method

DAY ONE

Thoroughly clean a large mason jar. Add in 200 g wholemeal flour.

In a clean jug, measure 200 ml tepid water, by adding cold tap water and adding a little boiled water from a kettle. Pour this into the jar and mix. Seal the jar and leave in a warm place for 24 hours.

DAY TWO

Pop open the lid and stir in 100 g more flour and 100 ml more tepid water. The ratio is very simple: however many grams of flour you put in, add in the same number of millilitres of water.

Reseal your jar and return it to its warm place.

DAY THREE

Pop the lid again and you should notice some bubbles and a slight tang beginning to develop. Your starter has begun to ferment! This is a good time to welcome it into your life with a name and a ceremonial bow: we named ours Doughreen.

Repeat the same step as for day two: add in 100 g flour and 100 ml water.

DAY FOUR

Your starter should now be bubbling happily and developing a fermented, fruity aroma. You

DID YOU KNOW?

Researchers believe sourdough's prebiotic composition and probiotic properties (see page 184) are responsible for making it easier to digest than bread fermented with brewer's yeast. Sourdough contains higher levels of antioxidants than other breads, while its lower phytic acid levels allow your body to absorb the nutrients it contains more readily. It is believed that sourdough fermentation may break down gluten better than baker's yeast, so sourdough's lower gluten content may also make it literally easier to stomach for anyone sensitive to gluten.

are now ready to bake bread with your living starter. You can use it in any bread recipe that calls for dried or fresh yeast.

To keep your starter going, continue to feed it every day or every other day (depending on how often you wish to make bread) with 50/100 g flour, and 50/100 ml water. I find it easiest to do this with a coffee measuring spoon – I add in 1 spoon flour and 1 spoon water every few days to keep the starter going. The fruity, fermented smell will continue to deepen over the next few days as your starter matures, provided you keep feeding it.

If you are going away or don't plan to use it for a while, you can freeze it in a tub or refrigerate your jar, feeding it once every four or five days. You can also freeze part of your starter – half, say – for use another time, or to give to a friend, to share your sourdough initiation. To top up your own starter if it's getting low, simply add a little more flour and water than usual – 150–200 g/ml – and it will soon revive. You can keep a starter going indefinitely.

FOR YOUR LOAF

Take 200 g of your starter and mix in a large mixing bowl with 250 ml tepid water. Add 400 g strong white flour and 1½ tsp salt. Mix together into a sloppy dough, using either your fingers or a wooden spoon.

Knead for 8–10 minutes until your dough is supple. Add a little extra flour if it's too sticky, or water if it's too stiff. Pour a little extra virgin olive oil over, place in an oiled bread tin and cover with a damp cloth. Leave in a warm place for 8–12 hours, by which time it should have grown in size.

Bake on the floor of your oven at 230°C for 30–40 minutes. Check it at 30 minutes. A golden crust will have formed. To check if it's ready, remove the loaf from the tin with oven gloves and tap the base with your fingernail. If it's ready, it should make a hollow sound. If it makes a doughy thud, return it to the oven for another 5–10 minutes. Remove from oven and leave to cool on a rack. Slice, serve and enjoy!

TROUBLESHOOTING

If nothing seems to be happening after three or four days, make sure the place where your jar is sitting is warm enough and give it another few days. A temperature of around 25–29°C is ideal, but this may not be possible in your home; aim to have it at 22°C or above if possible. If it is still lifeless, start again with a new batch of flour. Make sure the water is tepid when you add it (around 30°C is ideal) and the place you are storing it is warm. If any mould grows (this is uncommon), discard immediately.

Make sure you very carefully open the lid of your jar daily to release the pressure that has built up. When it is really active, you may need to do this two or three times a day. Some people prefer to keep theirs in a plastic box for this reason.

This is only a brief introduction; whole books are written on sourdough fermentation and baking. Enjoy experimenting with your ripening starter.

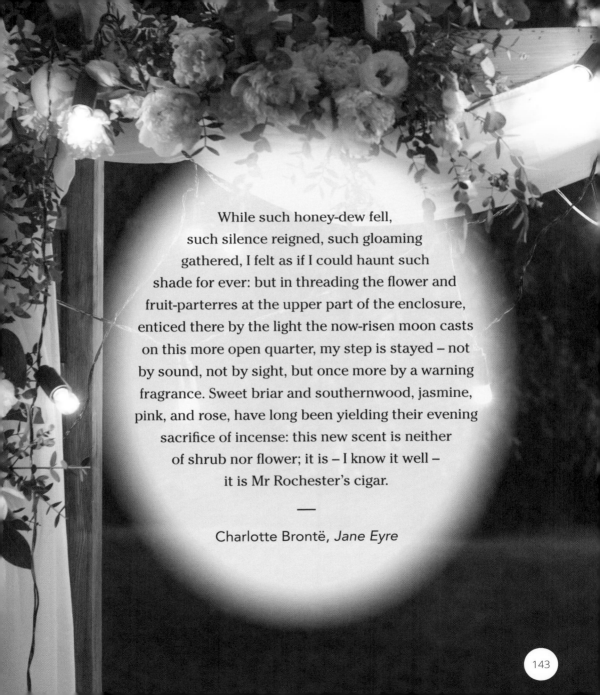

While such honey-dew fell,
such silence reigned, such gloaming
gathered, I felt as if I could haunt such
shade for ever: but in threading the flower and
fruit-parterres at the upper part of the enclosure,
enticed there by the light the now-risen moon casts
on this more open quarter, my step is stayed – not
by sound, not by sight, but once more by a warning
fragrance. Sweet briar and southernwood, jasmine,
pink, and rose, have long been yielding their evening
sacrifice of incense: this new scent is neither
of shrub nor flower; it is – I know it well –
it is Mr Rochester's cigar.

—

Charlotte Brontë, *Jane Eyre*

If you're interested in finding out more about our books,
find us on Facebook at Summersdale Publishers
and follow us on Twitter at @Summersdale.

www.summersdale.com

IMAGE CREDITS

Front cover images from top left: ciabatta © Oksana Mizina/Shutterstock.com; blue room © Arno Smit/Unsplash; flowers © look2you/Shutterstock.com; cottage © Annie Spratt/Unsplash; bike © Florencia Viadana/Unsplash; perfume bars © P-fotography/Shutterstock.com; lavender in jug © Juliya Zadonskaya/Shutterstock.com; floral pattern © VerisStudio/Shutterstock.com

Back cover images from top left: cottages © VictoriaSh/Shutterstock.com; wool © Shyntartanya/Shutterstock.com; pine cones © xuanhuongho/Shutterstock.com; tea and roses © Loverna Journey/Unsplash; flowers © nature photos/Shutterstock.com; logs © MomoShi/Shutterstock.com; apples © iravgustin/Shutterstock.com

p.4 – flowers in jug © Svetlana Gorbacheva/Shutterstock.com; flower in basket and watering can © Maria Evseyeva/Shutterstock.com; p.5 – cat and pumpkins © Svetlana Gorbacheva/Shutterstock.com; bread © Besedina Julia/Shutterstock.com; pp.6–7 © Daria Minaeva/Shutterstock.com; p.8 – blue flowers © Ulyana Khorunzha/Shutterstock.com; heart candles © Sunlike/Shutterstock.com; pebbles © naluwan/Shutterstock.com; daffodils © Africa Studio/Shutterstock.com; paper craft © MorganStudio/Shutterstock.com; bunting © Africa Studio/Shutterstock.com; p.10 © Anna Bogush/Shutterstock.com; p.11 – plates with seashells © Anna Bogush/Shutterstock.com; table setting © Watercolor_Art_Photo/Shutterstock.com; heart candles © Sunlike/Shutterstock.com; flowers in mugs © Antonova Ganna/Shutterstock.com; p.13 © Maren Winter/Shutterstock.com; p.14 © TaraPatta/Shutterstock.com; p.15 – rolls of fabric © macka/Shutterstock.com; scissors and thread © vi mart/Shutterstock.com; folded fabric © so_lizaveta/Shutterstock.com; pp.16–17 © totojang1977/Shutterstock.com; p.18 – candles © Africa Studio/Shutterstock.com; jar © Joanna Stankiewicz-Witek/Shutterstock.com; p.19 – oil © DUSAN ZIDAR/Shutterstock.com; plant © Oxana Denezhkina/Shutterstock.com; p.20 © otabaluk/Shutterstock.com; pp.22–23 – flowers in basket © Marina Zarova/Shutterstock.com; drying herbs © stockcreations/Shutterstock.com; bike with flowers © Lifestyle Travel Photo/Shutterstock.com; meadow with butterfly © lola1960/Shutterstock.com; plates © Daria Minaeva/Shutterstock.com; woman in meadow © Zolotarevs/Shutterstock.com; pp.24–25 – main background photo © DUSAN ZIDAR/Shutterstock.com; medium circle photo © aliasemma/Shutterstock.com; small circle photo © Laszlo Szelenczey/Shutterstock.com; pp.26–27 © angelakatharina/Shutterstock.com; p.28 © Protasov AN/Shutterstock.com; p.31 © Anna Chavdar/Shutterstock.com; p.32 © mythja/Shutterstock.com; p.33 © on_france/Shutterstock.com; p.34 © Alphonsine Sabine/Shutterstock.com; pp.36–37 – typewriter © Irra/Shutterstock.com; boots © Imfoto/Shutterstock.com; tyres © Toey Toey/Shutterstock.com; helmet © WIN12_ET/Shutterstock.com; flippers © topdigipro/Shutterstock.com; pp.38–39 © frankie's/Shutterstock.com; p.40 – flowers in bucket © VICUSCHKA/Shutterstock.com; jug © Smeerjewegproducties/Shutterstock.com; view through gate © Nicole Kwiatkowski/Shutterstock.com; flowers © U.Klinger/Shutterstock.com; sunset hut © Niar/Shutterstock.com; kitchen with fairy lights © NataliaLavrivNedashkivska/Shutterstock.com; pp.42–43 © natalia bulatova/Shutterstock.com; p.44 – lavender © B.G. Photography/Shutterstock.com; cutting lavender © Art_Maric/Shutterstock.com; p.47 – lavender bag © Jelena Yukka/Shutterstock.com; p.48 – glowing lights © Natali Zakharova/Shutterstock.com; fairy-light jar © tomertu/Shutterstock.com; p.49 – fairy lights © Nikolaev Mikhail/Shutterstock.com; lights in jar © tomertu/Shutterstock.com; p.51 © P-fotography/Shutterstock.com; pp.52-53 © shopplaywood/Shutterstock.com; p.54 © Lunov Mykola/Shutterstock.com; pp.56-57 – flowers © PannaPhoto/Shutterstock.com; woman among sunflowers © juliaap/Shutterstock.com; woman reading © PhotoNH/Shutterstock.com; table © gostua/Shutterstock.com; flowers in bucket © Anna Chavdar/Shutterstock.com; hat and wine glasses © Razbitnov/Shutterstock.com; p.59 – top left and bottom © lcrms/Shutterstock.com; top right © JurateBuiviene/Shutterstock.com; p.60 © Shelli Jensen/Shutterstock.com; p.62 © Oksana Mizina/Shutterstock.com; p.64 © Rimma Bondarenko/Shutterstock.com; p.67 © Marina Onokhina/Shutterstock.com; p.68 © MaxCab/Shutterstock.com; p.74 – bowls © Ulyana Khorunzha/Shutterstock.com; heart toast © Itummy/Shutterstock.com; marshmallows © Kiian Oksana/Shutterstock.com; kitchen sideboard © Leonova Iuliia/Shutterstock.com; butternut squash © Veronika Idiyat/Shutterstock.com; chestnuts © Karl Allgaeuer/Shutterstock.com; p.76 – flowers in jug © Chamille White/Shutterstock.com; pine cones © xuanhuongho/Shutterstock.com; p.77 © Tamotsu Ito/Shutterstock.com; p.78 © Subbotina Anna/Shutterstock.com; p.79 – bluebells © mj - tim photography/Shutterstock.com; trees © Creative Travel Projects/Shutterstock.com; p.81 – crumble © Peter OToole/Shutterstock.com; apples © iravgustin/Shutterstock.com; pp.82–83 © MomoShi/Shutterstock.com; p.84 – chess pieces © Plateresca/Shutterstock.com; playing cards © Eisfrei/Shutterstock.com; p.85 – film-related images and book case © Julia August/Shutterstock.com; book © Maltiase/Shutterstock.com; pp.86–87 – cat © svitlini/Shutterstock.com; picnic © Marina Bakush/Shutterstock.com; books in basket © Soloviova Liudmyla/Shutterstock.com; hands holding fruit © Yulia Grigoryeva/Shutterstock.com; mug © Beau Papier/Shutterstock.com; candles © Svetlana Lev/Shutterstock.com; p.89 © Irina Bort/Shutterstock.com; p.90 – hanging candle © Anna Demianenko/Shutterstock.com; candles © Maya Kruchankova/Shutterstock.com; p.92 – fabric © fieldwork/Shutterstock.com; beanies © lcrms/Shutterstock.com; p.95 wool © images72/Shutterstock.com; p.96 © Galiyah Assan/Shutterstock.com; pp.98–99 © irin-k/Shutterstock.com; p.101 © Alin Lyre/Shutterstock.com; p.102 © Fairy Lens/Shutterstock.com; p.103 – hands holding berries © Anton Watman/Shutterstock.com; blackthorn © Perutskyi Petro/Shutterstock.com; elderberries © T. Kimmeskamp/Shutterstock.com; p.105 © Christian Jung/Shutterstock.com; up.106 – plant © iravgustin/Shutterstock.com; petals © Emma manners/Shutterstock.com; p.107 – pebbles © naluwan/Shutterstock.com; leaves © iravgustin/Shutterstock.com; seashells © Hurghea Constantin/Shutterstock.com; p.108 – socks © NinaMalyna/Shutterstock.com; fairy lights © Nikolaev Mikhail/Shutterstock.com; heart on glass © Anton Watman/Shutterstock.com; chopping board © ptystockphoto/Shutterstock.com; houses © Julia Karo/Shutterstock.com; mug © catalina.m/Shutterstock.com; pp.110–111 © imnoom/Shutterstock.com; pp.112–113 © Nick_Nick/Shutterstock.com; p.114 – photo © Dmitry Sheremeta/Shutterstock.com; pp.114–115 – shavings illustration © SofiaV/Shutterstock.com; other three illustrations © Kostiantyn Fedorov/Shutterstock.com; pp.116–117 – winter flower © iravgustin/Shutterstock.com; mug and books © catalina.m/Shutterstock.com; bread © Anyango/Shutterstock.com; candles © Svetlana Lukienko/Shutterstock.com; fire wood © mervas/Shutterstock.com; mug on blanket © Svetlana Lukienko/Shutterstock.com; p.118 © mama_mia/Shutterstock.com; p.121 – top left © Kati Finell/Shutterstock.com; top right © Masson/Shutterstock.com; bottom © Kiian Oksana/Shutterstock.com; p.122 – fabric © MILA Zed/Shutterstock.com; mug cosy © morrowlight/Shutterstock.com; p.125 © Mostovyi Sergii Igorevich/Shutterstock.com; p.127 © leonori/Shutterstock.com; p.128 © Le Chernina/Shutterstock.com; p.132 – fabric © Marina Kutukova/Shutterstock.com; slippers © Nataliia Kuznetcova/Shutterstock.com; p.135 © Brum/Shutterstock.com; p.137 © Valerio Pardi/Shutterstock.com; pp.138–139 rug © FotoHelin/Shutterstock.com; chair © Kristen Prahl/Shutterstock.com; candle sticks © Rich T Photo/Shutterstock.com; mirror frames © Lynda Disher/Shutterstock.com; lab stools © Margarita R. Padilla/Shutterstock.com; p.140 © Zagorulko Inka/Shutterstock.com; p.143 © Andrii Oleksiienko/Shutterstock.com